This book belongs to

....

....

I celebrated
World Book Day® 2026
with this gift from my local
bookseller and What on Earth!

WORLD BOOK DAY®
World Book Day® champions
the fun of reading, because it
seriously improves lives. We want every
child and young person to read their
way and find reading fun. To find out more,
and for fun activities including video stories,
audiobooks and book recommendations,
visit worldbookday.com

World Book Day®
is a charity sponsored by
National Book Tokens.

CONTENTS

- WELCOME 5
- BABIES 6
- SMILES & FACES 8
- TEETH 10
- MUSCLES 12
- POO 14
- ASTRONAUTS 16
- FARTS 18
- FARM ANIMALS 20
- FACT FRENZY 22
- MEDICINE 24
- MOUTHS & TONGUES 26
- SNOT 28
- DINOSAURS 30
- DANCES 32
- MIDDLE AGES 34
- FACT FRENZY 36
- MUSIC 38
- CATS 40
- FACT FRENZY 42
- FEET 44
- FOOD 46
- KINGS & QUEENS 48
- BATH TIME 50
- OCEAN 52
- SLEEP & DREAMS 54
- COLOURS 56
- OLDIES 58

>Welcome to Funny FACTopia!

Join me on a trail through one hundred hilarious, mind-blowing and bizarre facts. But WATCH OUT! Every fact is connected to the next one in the most bizarre and surprising ways. Jump from facts about **poo** to facts about **astronauts**, and from facts about **snot** to facts about **dinosaurs**...

And there isn't just one trail through this book. See how the path branches so you can travel to a totally different (but still connected) part of FACTopia. As you do so, remember that the most important thing is to follow whatever fascinates you most. Have your mind blown away with wonder as you discover that the real world is far more amazing than anything you can make up! ....>

Christopher Lloyd

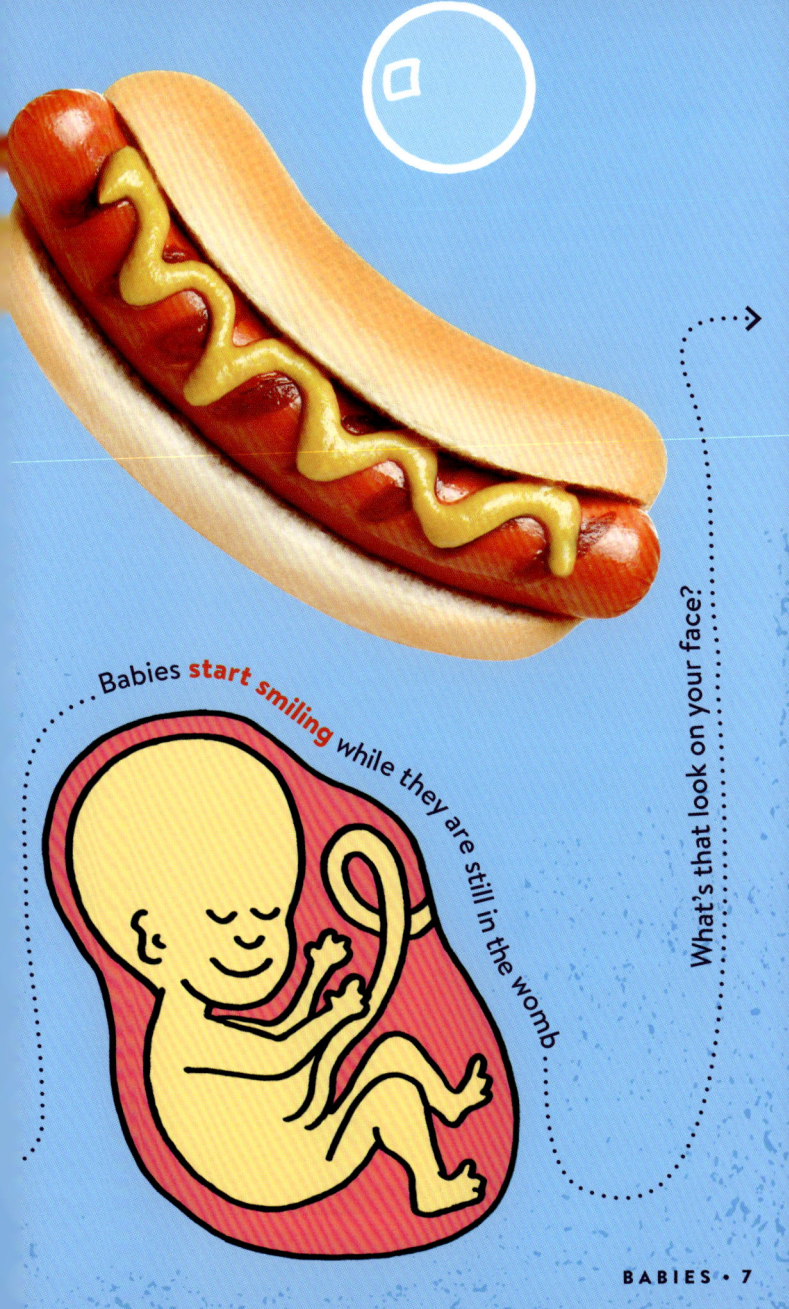

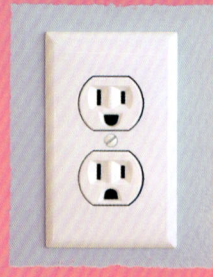

The word pareidolia (*pair-uh-doh-lee-uh*) describes the way we sometimes **see faces**, or other things, in random objects or images.

Terrific teeth

Sometimes chimpanzees smile and **show their teeth** to apologise to other chimps

SMILES & FACES • 9

One hundred million years ago, **birds had teeth**.

Rabbits' teeth **keep growing** for their whole lives

The **hardest stuff** in the human body is the coating on your

TEETH

Inside the body

Snails have **thousands of teeth**

Beavers have **orange teeth**

Cool colours

Go to page 56

If you can control your auricular (aw-ri-kyuh-ler) muscles you can wiggle your ears.

There are no muscles inside your fingers.

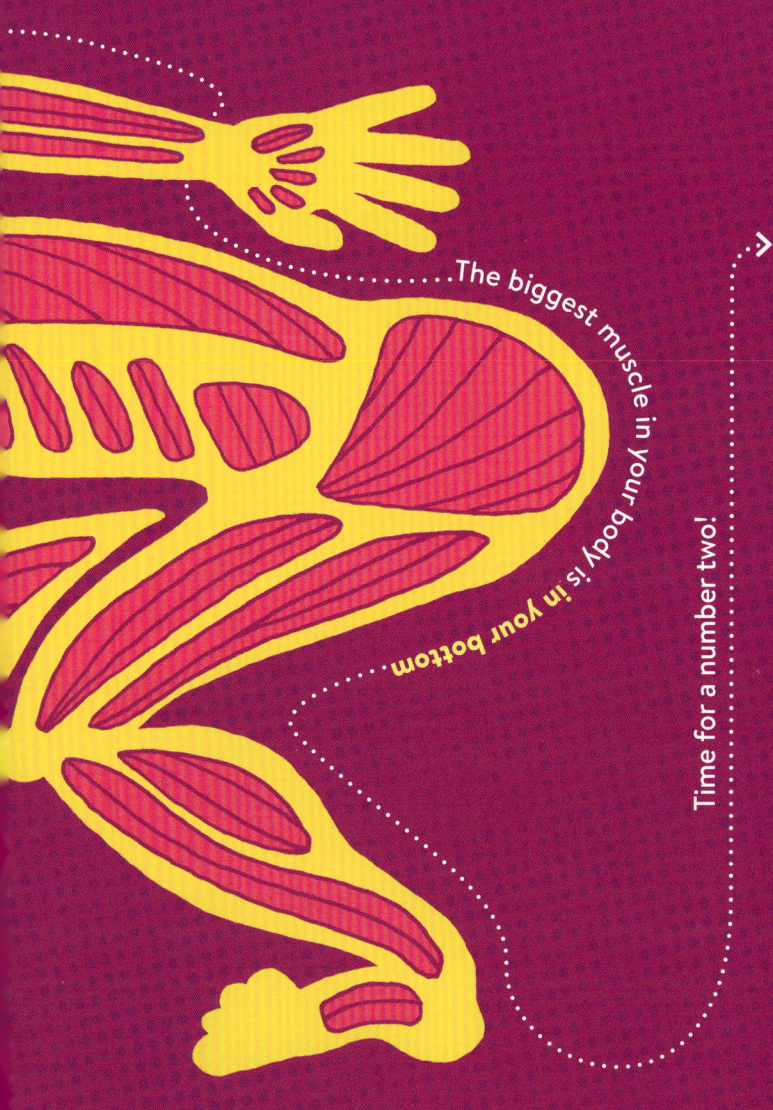

Astronauts once **baked cookies in space.** The cookies took 2 HOURS to bake in the special space oven.

One spacesuit costs more than a **lifetime supply of pizza.**

A SHEEP, A COCKEREL AND A DUCK

were the first passengers ever to fly in a hot air balloon.

Another no-brainer

A chicken's brain is partly inside its neck. Because of this, one chicken survived a whole year **without a head**.

FARM ANIMALS • 21

Jellyfish have no **brain**.

When an object is pulled through a black **hole**, it stretches out like a piece of **spaghetti**. This is called spaghettification.

One type of reptile is only as wide as a piece of **spaghetti**: it's the world's smallest **snake**!

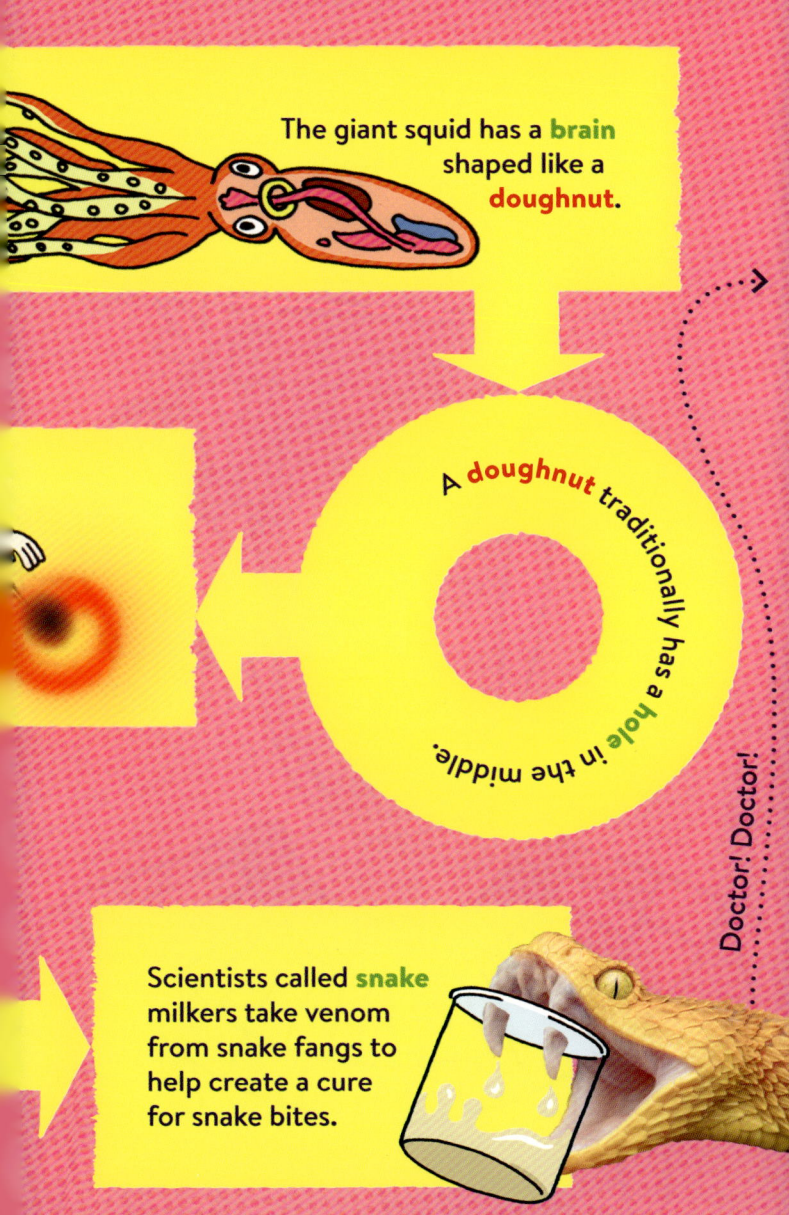

The giant squid has a **brain** shaped like a **doughnut**.

A **doughnut** traditionally has a *hole in the middle*.

Doctor! Doctor!

Scientists called **snake** milkers take venom from snake fangs to help create a cure for snake bites.

Go to page 34

That's medieval!

One Irish legend says you can cure a toothache by putting a **frog in your mouth**

Open wide!

Doctors used **slug soup** to treat certain poisons in the Middle Ages

An old British cure for a sore throat involved wrapping **sweaty socks** around your neck

MEDICINE • 25

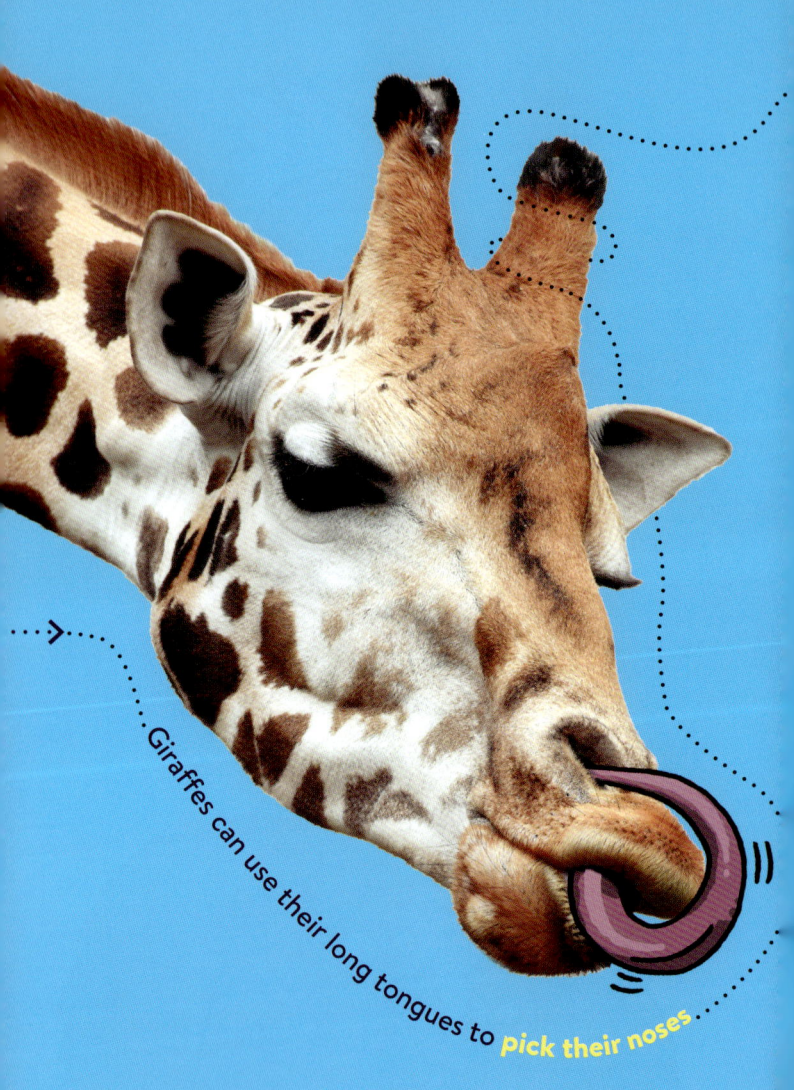

Bees perform a '**waggle dance**' to tell other bees where flowers are.

Poo-rolling dung beetles sometimes dance on top of their ball of poo.

32 • DANCES

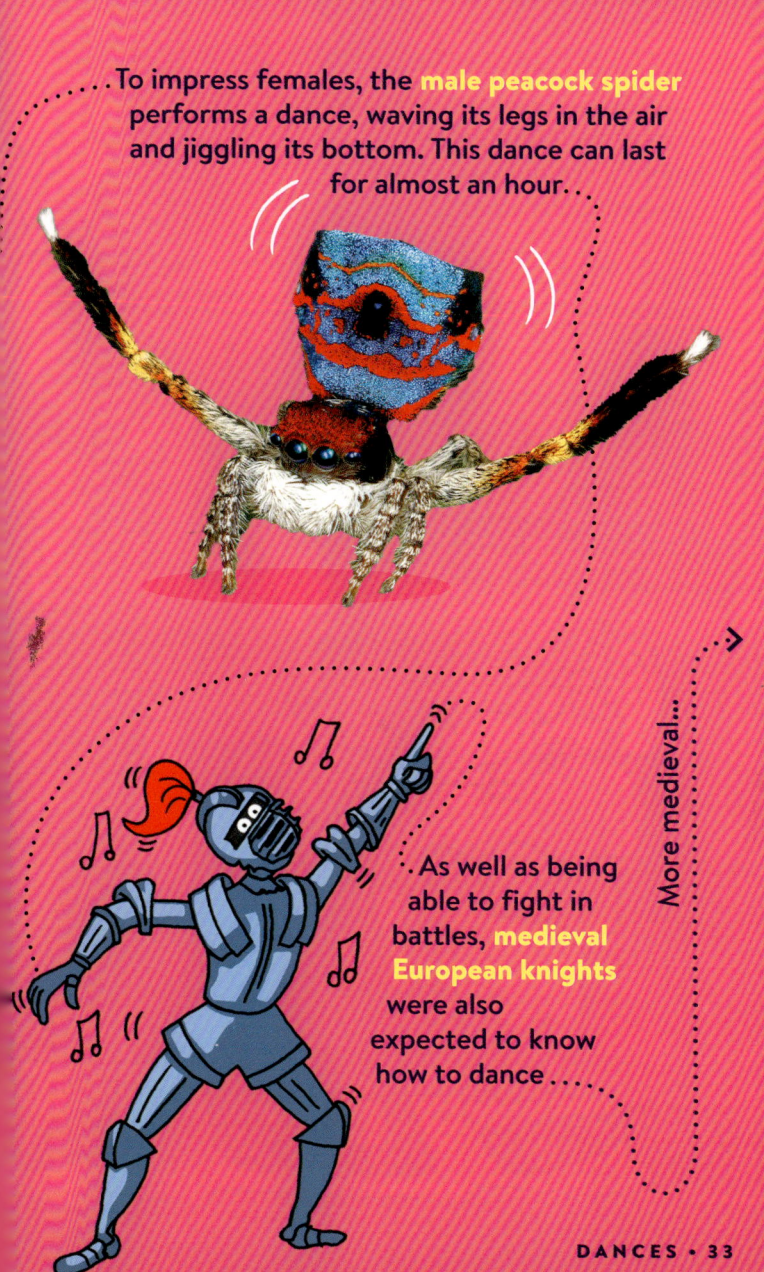

Some sand dunes 'sing' – scientists think the **sounds** are caused by the sand grains moving around.

Rabbits and guinea pigs are coprophages (*kop-ruh-fay-jiz*): animals that eat their own **poo**.

The bright pink **poo** of Adelie penguins can be seen from **space**.

The rumbling **sounds** your body makes when it's **hungry** are called **BORBORYGMI** (*bore-bore-ig-mee*).

French emperor Napoleon Bonaparte was once attacked – and defeated – by a group of **hungry rabbits**.

In **space**, there is no **SOUND**.

It's too quiet!

More purr-fect facts

One musician created songs **specifically for cats**.

Scientists can tell how **old** a whale is from its earwax.

Archaeologists discovered a 50,000-year-**old** fossil of human **poo**.

Of all animals alive today, the one with the **longest** neck is the **giraffe**.

A **burp** that lasted over a minute is the **longest** ever recorded!

Giraffes suck on animal **bones** for extra nutrients.

Humans usually **poo** up to three times per day. **Mice** can poo up to 75 times per day!

Mice can't **BURP**.

More than half the **bones** in your body are in your hands and feet.

Step this way

...A skunk will **stomp its front feet** as a warning that it is about to spray....

Antarctic emperor penguins **rock back and forth on their heels** to stop their feet from freezing......

Geckos are able to **change the stickiness of their feet** – they can turn it on and off.

A man from the UK once set a world record by using his toes to crush **60 eggs** in one minute.

When a fly walks across your food, it is **tasting the flavour** with its feet.

Mmmm, yummy!

Go to page 10

Brush you r teeth!

One of the inventors of the *candy floss* machine was a dentist.

46 • FOOD

CHEWING GUM IS A FULL-TIME JOB FOR A **GUMOLOGIST**, WHO RESEARCHES AND TESTS GUM AND EVEN CREATES NEW FLAVOURS.

Queen Elizabeth I impressed foreign visitors with **gingerbread men** made to look like them.

By royal invitation

Some dessert companies have professional **ice-cream scientists**

FOOD • 47

Go to page 30

Discover the dinos

The largest known **fossilised dinosaur footprint** ever discovered was about the size of a large bathtub.

In 1992, **28,000 bath toys**, including rubber ducks, beavers

Find some space

...The planet **Saturn would float** in a bathtub full of water, if there were one big enough...

Dive in

and turtles, fell out of a ship into the Pacific Ocean...

BATH TIME • 51

Meerkats **sleep in a pile**

Rabbits can sleep with their **eyes open**.

Face the facts

Go to page 8

54 • SLEEP & DREAMS

Chameleons **change the colour** of their skin to help them cool down or warm up.

56 • COLOURS

...The world's longest-living land animal is

Jonathan,

a tortoise that was born before the petrol car was invented!

Welcome to FACTopia, where each fact leads on to the next in endlessly entertaining ways!

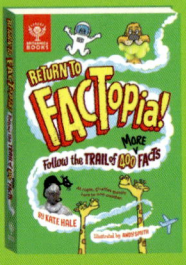
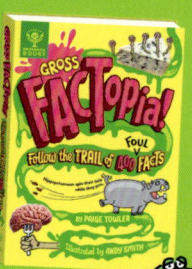
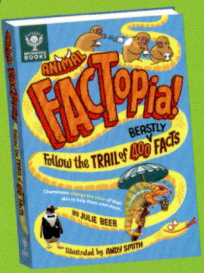
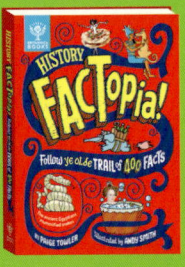
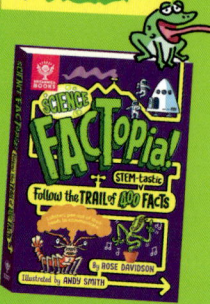
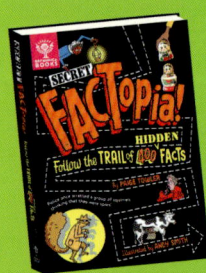
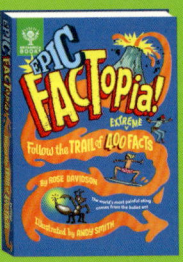
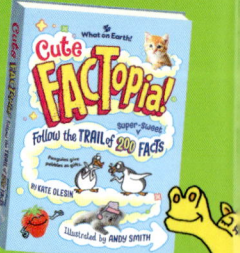

Find out more about FACTopia and take the quiz here:

www.whatonearthbooks.com/funnyfactopia/

What on Earth!

If you enjoyed this book, you might like *What on Earth! Magazine*. Filled with astounding facts, spectacular photos and illustrations, fascinating true-life stories, as well as quizzes, puzzles, activities and jokes, it is perfect for curious kids.

To find out more, visit:
www.whatonearthmag.com/mag

The reading for fun charity

Reading's a rollercoaster, enjoy the ride!

Just like the best rides, when one book ends, you can't wait to hop on the next. So turn the page and get ready to go!

SPONSORED BY
NATIONAL BOOK tokens

What's your next read?

When one book ends, there are loads more to choose from.
Head to your nearest library or bookshop and pick your next read!

Here are three simple ways to make reading more fun.

1. Choice

Choose a book you want to read.

2. Time

Set aside time to read every day, or whenever you can.

3. Together

Read and share books together.

For more ideas on making reading fun, go to **worldbookday.com**

What on Earth!

What on Earth Books is an imprint of What on Earth Publishing
The Black Barn, Wickhurst Farm, Leigh, Tonbridge, Kent, UK, TN11 8PS
30 Ridge Road Unit B, Greenbelt, Maryland, 20770, United States

First published in the United Kingdom in 2026

Text copyright © 2026 What on Earth Publishing Ltd. and Britannica inc.
Illustrations copyright © 2021, 2022, 2023, 2024, 2025, 2026 Andy Smith

World Book Day ® is a registered UK trademark owned by World Book Day Limited.
The associated logo is the subject of a pending UK trademark application. Registered charity number 1079257 (England and Wales) Registered company number 03783095 (UK).

Image credits: Front cover: GlobalP/iStockphoto; p.7 Valentina Razumova/Dreamstime; p.8 Cedric Leresche/ Dreamstime (wood); Paul David Galvin/Getty Images (cheese grater); Juan Silva/Getty Images (plug socket); Natalie Bellos (coat hanger); Vovalis/Dreamstime (pepper); Marcy Schrum/Dreamstime (banana); Michelle K Wood/Dreamstime (puddle); Natalie Bellos (cake); Nathan Graham Photography/Shutterstock (toilet); Richard Van Der Spuy/Dreamstime (can); p.10 jimmyjamesbond/iStockphoto; p.11 t Freder/iStockphoto; p.11 b Itsik Marom/Alamy; p.14 eriklam/123RF; pp.14–15 Carol Buchanan/Dreamstime; p.16 Vincent Besnault/Getty Images; p.17 Rastan/Dreamstime; p.18 Joe Sohm/Dreamstime; p.20 Eric Isselee/Shutterstock; p.21 ekina/iStockphoto; p.23 Mark Kostich/iStockphoto; p.24 Khosrock/Dreamstime; p.26 Lin Backer/Dreamstime; p.28 NAPA/Shutterstock; pp.30–31 JoeLena/Getty Images; p.32 phichak/Adobe Stock; p.33 Robbie Goodall/Getty Images; p.34 Michael C. Gray/Shutterstock; pp.34–35 tandemich/Shutterstock; p.38 DEV IMAGES/Getty Images; p.39 Akimasa Harada/Getty Images; p.40 FOTOGRAPHICA INC./iStockphoto; p.41 Eric Isselee/Shutterstock; p.43 GlobalP/iStock.com; p.45 t Eric Isselee/Shutterstock; p.45 b Liubov Mernaya Charignon/Dreamstime; p.47 Prostock-Studio/iStockphoto; p.48 Aleksandra Lande/Dreamstime; p.49 Alexandra Rus/Dreamstime; p.51 Nerthuz/iStockphoto; p.52 scubaluna/iStockphoto/Getty Images; p.53 Pamela Hodson/Dreamstime; p.54 Sharomka/Shutterstock; p.55 mokuden photos/Getty Images; p.56 PetlinDmitry/Shutterstock; p.57 David Acosta Allely/Dreamstime; pp.58–59 Morphart Creation/Shutterstock.

All rights reserved. No part of this publication may be reproduced or transmitted in any form or by any means, electronic or mechanical, including photocopying, recording, or any information storage or retrieval system, without permission in writing from the publishers. Requests for permission to make copies of any part of this work should be directed to info@whatonearthbooks.com.

Created by Christopher Lloyd and Kate Olesin,
with contributions from Paige Towler, Julie Beer and Rose Davidson
Edited by Judy Barratt
Designed by Lawrence Morton
Illustrated by Andy Smith

Andy Smith has asserted his right to be identified as illustrator under the Copyright, Designs and Patents Act 1988.

Staff for this book: Nancy Feresten, Managing Director; Natalie Bellos, Publisher; Charka Stout, Assistant Editor; Andy Forshaw, Art Director; Nell Wood, Senior Designer; Sian Smith, Production Manager

A CIP catalogue record for this book is available from the British Library

ISBN: 9781804661901

EU Authorised Representative: Easy Access System Europe - Mustamäe tee 50, 10621 Tallinn, Estonia, gpsr.requests@easproject.com.

Printed in China
CCO/Shenzhen, China/10/2025

10 9 8 7 6 5 4 3 2 1

whatonearthbooks.com